B Beliefs

Beliefs shape characters and behaviors! The opinion you had in the past, the set of perceptions you have formed, are called Beliefs! You have to Notice and Identify what feeling is pulling you down. When the feeling that sabotage you appears (what time it occurs and under what circumstances are your limiting beliefs jumping into your mind?) Most beliefs have been formed when we were younger (from your parents, teachers, friends). A strict environment, the Rejection or the Deprivation you felt, are feelings you are carrying with you for the rest of your life. NOT ANY MORE! Try to understand when a belief is coming to your mind. Then keep distance from the event and take different action. Act like you are facing the ideal scenario you had in your mind!

When the limiting beliefs appear? Perception.	How that beliefs Sabotage myself?	Change my old belief with a new one (Find a positive outcome. New Evidence to replace the old limiting belief)

C Challenges

Challenge yourself in a daily bases and raise your standards!
By provoking yourself, you are enforced to try harder. You train your brain on how to react in any situation. Your actions and what you are doing in your life are based on what you believe you are. You have to be consistent with yourself so all of your actions are based on your beliefs.

Find out what I am scared of and do it consistently.	Dedicate few minutes each day to physical-spiritual and mental exercise	Face challenges in a way to achieve my goal and write a solution for each challenge.

A few Words about myself…

I am the founder of James Coaching Educational Academy & Therapy Centre and which is active in the field of Personal Improvement, Neuro-linguistic Programming, Life Coaching, Counseling and other techniques and strategies for Personal Development and achievement of goals.

I am a Sales and business consultant since 2006 in Greece and Cyprus. I am a shareholder in Investia Greece & Lithos Investments based in Athens.
Due to my deep love for books and literature I began writing books from an early age and I have been awarded in International contests and I won many Pan-Hellenic Prizes as well as Distinctions in Literature, Essays and Poetry.
I also become a member (Co-Founder and Owner) of a Publishing House.
I am the Inspiration & Founder of Humanitarian and Charitable Internet Foundation: Invest In Humanity.
My love for books and advisory dialectics was born from an early age when I started writing my first book on my grandfathers old typewriter.
After my first attempt to publish a psychological novel my works were awarded and distinguished by the Pan-Hellenic Writers' Union, literary journals and International Poetry Competitions. I am also writing in newspapers and magazines on self-improvement techniques and personal development issues.

The themes of my books and my theories are rooted in psychology, sociology are anthropocentric and my goal is to examine human psychology and the inexhaustible power that conceals within.

I studied dental technician in Athens and I have been involved in this field for several years. Then my interest began to turn to the art of sales resulting is working as a Sales Consultant and Advisor in Real Estate business for over eleven years in Greece, Cyprus and abroad.

I attended lectures and seminars in Life Coaching & Business Coaching in Greece and abroad. I have also been certified as a Life Coach, have Certificate of Coaching, Mentoring, a Diploma of Master Practitioner & NLP Master Coach (Neuro-Linguistic Programming) and other specialized training titles on the Advisory and Coaching field. I have dealt with the technique of spiritual concentration, Theta Waves, EFT, meditation and yoga.

Concluding, I just want to tell you that there are problems and obstacles in our lives but our attitude and our actions can exterminate them. Through difficulties and failures the power to fulfill your goals is born ... and these power reserves within you!

"Learn again the alphabet of Happiness"

 Awareness

Awareness is the observation and understanding without criticism and comparison! Awareness is silent. Is a state of consciousness where you can observe yourself as a third observer, as if you were looking yourself from a distance. Observe you body, observe your mind and your thoughts…

Having Awareness is half of the therapy, Psychologists say. Having awareness, means that you are distancing yourself and you understand clearly and deeply all the facts in a given situation.

Write today some cases that you have been adherent and intent at the present time. Observer at "Now". Consciousness!

Where have I been?	What did I "see"? Awareness	How did I feel?

D Determination

Determination. Important decisions that have been taken have changed the future of a man, a family, a business, a society, the whole of Humanity! A Crucial decision requires courage. You have to be self-confident, strong and patient. Be idle and remember that you can not please everyone and always! A determined person knows exactly where he or she is on the road to success. You always see a solution in any problem and how to pass the obstacles. Success does not just happen out of nowhere, it needs a irreversible and final strategy-plan.

Consider various areas of my life, such as my career, relationship, health, passions, etc. What would each of these areas be like in its best possible scenario?	I took that final decision… and I will not deviate.	What obstacles may I face? Am I ready to deal with any threat?

E   **Emotions**

Positive emotions have a powerful effect on your brain and body. Without Emotions & Feelings you would lose every trace of passion you have within you. Thoughts charged with emotions can be very powerful indeed. Negative emotions stifle the benefits of positive emotions and negative feelings don't improve the way we manage the bad things coming in life. People are happy because they have developed the resources to deal with life's challenges. Positive emotions strengthen the brain and keep mind and neurons in a healthy state.

The Negative emotions I am feeling	Now Replaced the negative emotion with a positive emotion. Think a time you are proud of. Thing a time of Gratitude, of Love, Of Joy and Happiness	Describe my new Feelings

F   **Fear**

False Evidence Appearing Real is the Acronym of Fear and is absolutely right! You make terrible scenarios, you create horrifying stories about something that does not exist. You are spending your energy and your time on something that is not real… The Future! Make your Fear your ally in order to evolve yourself. Most of the things you are afraid of will NEVER happen!

Identify my FEAR	What is the best thing-Result if I try to do that and What is the worst thing could happen?	Is that FEAR useful to me, to my life or does it pull me down to the bottom?

G Gratitude

Gratitude attracts what we want to achieve. Law of attraction says that you will attract the things you think about and the things you focus on. Being more grateful makes you happier and more optimistic. Gratitude is more than just saying thank you or please and have good manners. It is related to the pleasure of what you receive and the recognition of the positive things that come in your way. When you are grateful you are pleased and you are able to appreciate the good things you have without considering them as granted. It is a feeling that spontaneously emerges from within you. However, it's not just an emotional reaction, it is a state of mind!

Make a list of things I am grateful for right now. Little things in Life (Sun, Air, Breath, Family, Personal and professional…)	Say thanks for everything I have, A big thank you for being alive	Allow myself to feel good about these things.

H  Halt

Distancing! When a limiting belief comes to your head, HALT! See the situation as a third observer. Take the time to see the situation more clearly. Observe the event and try to find realistic and clear solutions.

Halt from a difficult Situation or from making a decision	See clearly, Observe, Study, Evaluate and judge the current situation	ACTION! After distancing, take action. Take risks and decisions

I   **Inspiration**

Inspiration makes things move in life. Inspiration and Motivation is leverage. It puts us in action from inaction! Inspiration is a positive driver for Success! Inspiration concerns every person who wants to be alive and creativity is what keeps us alive! Life without inspiration is like having a man who does not "breathe"!

"Inspiration exists, but it has to find you working." —*Pablo Picasso*

I see my Dream-Goal and commit to its implementation	Write positive thoughts about my Goal	See the big picture. Describe feelings of my Success

 J   Joy

Discover things in your life that give you Joy because is one of the most important elements in your life. Joy is something we all want to experience. Joy is the emotional state that increases the energy of life.

"Happiness is not something ready made. It comes from your own actions."
Dalai Lama

When am I in a negative state (Thoughts, anger, sad)…	Think about something that offers me Joy, Smile, Play, Dance, Sing, walk etc…	I keep that picture in my mind and reverse my state

K Knowledge

Knowledge is utmost importance. It helps you understand each step better. It helps you understand other people and gives you Confidence, Power, Certainty and Safety. Spend Every day at least half an hour in learning something new. Read a book, listen to an Audio-book, attend seminars and webinars, master in a subject that interests you, learn something important to you, Work Harder for yourself!

What did I learn today?	For what reason I needed that lesson?	How can I use it? This lesson is useful for…

L Love

Love is the Quintessence of life, is the essence of life. We all need love. We all have to give love. Love is that innate power that motivates us to build relationships, to be more creative, to be happier!

"To love someone is nothing, to be loved by someone is something, but to be loved by the one you love is everything"
Bill Russell

I love…	Reason I love that (person-Situation-Pet-work-personal) is…	It gives me…

M Method

Create a plan for your Goal. Find all the ways, all the methods that will lead you to Success. Knowledge, Understanding and Dreaming are nothing without a PLAN. You have to make a list of all of the thoughts running through your head and place them in order. The whole process is based on methods you are using to achieve your Goal!

My first Plan is… (strategy)	Second method and how to use it….	The Final Result is…

N   **Notice**

Notice everything and everyone as carefully as possible. By using this method (in NLP) you deactivate The Default Mode Network. This network is responsible for your negative thoughts, for your anxiety, for your pessimistic scenarios that your brain creates. By being Present and Noticing (Narrow and Broad), by focusing on a specific thing in the room or noticing the general picture, listening to a specific sound or the total of sounds, then you deactivate the Default Mode Network which is responsible for your mind's babbling. Feel your body, notice yourself, feel the air, be present.

I notice a sound…	I notice something I am seeing…	Notice how I am feeling (sitting on a chair or running, or walking etc)

O   **Outcome**

Everything you do in life should bring you closer in achieving your Goal! Set small goals and always reward yourself in every small victory! Set a SMART Goal. That means that it has to be Specific, Measurable, Achievable, Realistic and Time based. Stay focused on your target and do not deviate from your goal. Commitment! While you are committed you will do what ever it takes to succeed. You will learn everything you need to know, you will hear everything you need to hear, you will practice as much as you can, you will do everything needed to get where you want.

What is my goal? What are the results I want?	Why do I want it? Why is so important to me? Why am I excited?	What do I need to do? What actions do I need to plan in order to achieve it?

P Procrastination

"Leave it for tomorrow", "It's ok I will do it later", "I am not ready, better leave it for when I will be in a better condition or better prepared"… And this future never comes! Systematic transfer of liabilities in future time. When that happens often is the most common way to sabotage yourself. The fear of failure and the things we are afraid of are the basic reasons for procrastination. Do not Procrastinate. Do it now! Why not you? Why not now?

I understand I procrastinate on that issue (Write the issue)	My obligations/tasks for today…	Classification of my Obligations…

Q Qualifications

It is very important to know what Qualifications you have. Qualifications will differentiate you from others. If you have all the qualifications needed to achieve your goal and to be Successful is a huge advantage. If you do not have the qualifications needed then you have to acquire them. Qualifications will make you pass to the next level. Keep in mind that the market is very demanding!

Qualifications I have and are advantages on the market (Competition)	Qualifications I do not have but are necessary to acquire…	What actions I have to take to acquire the qualifications (skills) I need?

R Resistance

Interferences are innumerable, they block you, deconstruct you and redirect you from Success. Resist! Try to stay focused on what you want to achieve. Maybe sometimes you are bored, you do not want to do anything but sit on the sofa, watch tv, spend hours and hours on Social Media etc… Push Yourself to take Action! By pushing yourself to take action, all of your neurons are getting stronger and by repeating that procedure or the action you keep your brain in a perfect condition. Try to change your old rituals and habits and create new daily routines that will help you achieve your Dream!

I recognize what distracts me...	I am creating new Rituals and habits that will get me closer to what I want to achieve...	My new list...

S Specific

Be specific on what you want! No matter how good your boat is, if you do not know your exact destination, there are two possibilities: Either you reach an unknown coast or you are drown by the waves… Have a Clear, Specific and Identified Goal, so you will be able to give the correct coordinates to your Mind's GPS that will lead you to Success.

What do I want to accomplish?	Who is involved and Where (in which field?)	Analytical characteristics of my specific Goal

T Time Management

You protect all of your valuable items. You do not want somebody to take from you a precious gift or steal from you all your money. Then why are you stealing from yourself? Why are you wasting the most precious gift you have… Your time! Be careful with whom you spend your time with. Be careful with whom you are busy and on what actions you spend your time. You can buy a house, you can buy a car, you can by a cell phone but you Can't buy time! All of your actions must have deadlines and scale from high importance to insignificant.

Important and Urgent thing to do…	Not so Important	Insignificant – Minors (task allocation)

U   **Understanding**

Understand your feelings and not be blind to see, feel and accept all your feelings and specially the negative ones. If you ignore your negative feelings you will never understand them and you will never be cured from the situation you are in. Understand the others with empathy. C. Rogers said that Empathy is the key of mind reading. Is the best way to understand and feel an other person's problems, obstacles, issues and emotions. Getting in the shoes of others is the key for helping yourself be more objective, distant and selfish.

I thank myself for that I have. I understand my feelings and recognize the negative emotions…(write) so I can control them	How I would feel if I was in his/her position? (empathy)	I have Self-awareness, emotions, self-esteem and self-confidence and I express me feelings…

V   Visualization

Visualization is the most common secret of all the successful people!
Use Visualization in a daily bases. For a few minutes each day, take the time
to illustrate the acquisition of your goal. Visualize it. Close your eyes and live
in the state of the desired outcome. Use all of your senses. Hear, See, Taste,
Smell, Feel the Success! Your brain can not separate reality from imagination.
With Visualization you train your brain to choose which direction it needs to
follow!

Visualize my Desired state	Use all of my senses and imagine I am in a state of success	How do I feel?

 Worries

Keep your mind clear. Mindfulness and not Mindful! Do not worry for the future, do not worry for the past. The future does not exist and the past is gone! When you fill your mind with regrets, failures of the past, negative moments or you feed your brain with anxiety and fear about the future the only thing you manage to do is strengthen and multiply those negative feelings and you lose the miracle life, the present! Today!

Is my worry realistic? Is it true? Can I do something about the problem (solve it, control it)?	Make a list of all the possible solutions I can think of.	Accept the worry and feel safe. Practice mindfulness (Allow emotions to be present without judgment. Practice naming of emotions: "joy," "anger,", Notice body sensations, focus on your breathing)

 Plore

X-plore yourself (explore yourself) and discover your advantages and disadvantages. You have to know that Curiosity is one of the seven steps to Genius (Leonardo Da Vinci). Be curious like a child. Be curious to create passion and thirst for knowledge. Never drown your need for curiosity! Explore all the fields of your life.

"Search is the beginning of wisdom." Socrates!

Being curious for things I want to develop and I want to learn	Answers I received	What does that thing-that lesson mean to me?

Y You

Ultimate Power is hidden within you! We often spend time and energy worthlessly in situations that do not concern you, in situations that you can not control. Only You have the key leading to your happiness and that key is hidden deep inside you. Your potentials are limitless. Your Capabilities are so Powerful and the only thing you have to do it is to find out that power! Thank yourself and accept the facts you can not change.

I am grateful for the obstacles I have faced (name them) because they have made me stronger	I accept that (write an issue you had to face, or a feeling that blocks you) Because this is a part of my beautiful life.	I have the Ultimate Power to Do…

Z   Zone

Get out from your comfort Zone! Escape from you Comfort Zone! Before you perceive and understand enything you see, hear, or feel, your brain has already checked and recognized your state of affairs and this is done automatically and subconsciously for your own good. For your "safety". Your "safety" is what you have been accustomed to doing! You safe is your prison! Get out of those limits that keep you captive! Experimenting, Rischering, Trying for your goal, and avoiding a vicious circle. With the new effort, with new learning and new experience, you also strengthen your brain's neurons (Neuroplasticity-Symptoms-Neurogenesis). Life begins where the comfort zone is over!

Things make me feel safe (Things want me to have the control, not to risk anything but staying in my comfort zone!)	If I do not manage to get rid of this feeling (I'm writing the state-feeling makes me feel safe) then I'll stay ... (I'm writing the stuck state: Routine-Stagnation)	If I get rid of this anxiety (stuck state) that keeps me imprisoned in my comfort zone, then I will do the following greatly things:

www.ingramcontent.com/pod-product-compliance
Lightning Source LLC
Chambersburg PA
CBHW031915270726
48655CB00003BA/1299